THE RECIPES OF THE

Five Brothers

VOLUME II

Five Brothers One Passion

The Recipes of the Five Brothers ~ Volume II

Book Design:	Bart Goodell
Photography:	Jeff Weir
Writer/Editor:	Leah Rosch
Recipe Development:	Lynn Foley
	Rosemary Smalberg
Food Styling:	Michael DiBeneditto
Prop Styling:	Sylvia Lachter
Hand Lettering:	Bernard Maisner
Creative Direction:	Jeff Brall
Digital Production:	Rich Graham

Many thanks to all of these individuals who helped in making this
book a reality; Julie Ying, Betsy Floyd, Lori Zoppel, Larry Kadish,
Gail Young, Renée Tannenbaum and Jerry Simpson.

ISBN 0-9655889-1-2

Printed in China

A SANDY BOTTOM PRESS DESIGN

*L'amore per la buona tavola
é amore per la vita*

A passion for food is a passion for life

Contenuto

Introduzione

THE PERENNIAL NEW BEGINNING, SPRING IS THE ONE SEASON THAT CAN NEVER COME FAST ENOUGH—BOTH HERE AND in Tuscany. Spring is our psychic reward for having survived nature's hibernation. The days grow lighter, the weather kinder, as sunshine conspires with rain showers to coax out of their long sleep the first crop of tender vegetables—most notably, asparagus, artichokes, fava beans, baby carrots, and sweet green onions. In fact, more than relying on the calendar or warming trends, Italians trust those first asparagus sightings as real proof that spring has arrived. Salad leaves, particularly arugula and dandelion greens, are also flavorful harbingers of the season, followed later by the first blush of strawberries.

This is why in Tuscany spring is nowhere more welcome than in la cucina, the kitchen. Because it's there that nature's new harvest provides the fresh and flavorful ingredients for which Tuscan cooking is famous. The menus and recipes that follow take their inspiration from the venerable traditions of Tuscany's springtime cuisine. Yet, with their emphasis on fresh produce and simple, elegant preparations, these recipes fit perfectly with today's pared-down cooking and entertaining styles.

And if springtime in Tuscany is marked by the lush transformation of landscapes, the season is also greeted with a generous, and contagious, spirit of hospitality. There, as here, it's suddenly easier to host spontaneous get-togethers. Everyone, it seems, is more than ready to trade cabin fever for spring fever.

So, consider inviting friends over for an informal Sunday night supper or a special, leisurely brunch. Or host a fancy dinner for the extended family and close friends; the Neoclassic Dinner Party is certain to satisfy sophisticated palates. Whatever your pleasure, take advantage of spring's vegetables at their peak. One thing's for sure: they'll be gone again before you know it. ❧

Colazione di benvenuto alla primavera

SALUTATIONS OF SPRING BRUNCH

*This light, meatless menu combines ease and elegance in equal parts.
The asparagus frittata (an Italian omelette) is quintessential spring. Choosing
between the two pasta dishes will be no mean feat—they're both scrumptious.
And in conclusion, one of Italy's favorite springtime desserts—nothing could
be simpler and more palate-pleasing. Serves six.*

FRITTATA DI ASPARAGI
asparagus frittata

LINGUINE PRIMAVERA
linguine with spring vegetables
—— *or* ——
PENNE ALLA PUTTANESCA
penne puttanesca

INSALATA VERDE MISTA
mixed green salad

FRAGOLE ALL'ACETO BALSAMICO
strawberries in balsamic vinegar

linguine with spring vegetables

Frittata di asparagi

ASPARAGUS FRITTATA

Serve hot right from the skillet or at room temperature, sliced into wedges or bite-sized squares. Versatility only adds to this dish's appeal.

2 CUPS WATER	¼ TEASPOON SALT
½ POUND FRESH ASPARAGUS, TRIMMED AND CUT INTO 1-INCH PIECES	¼ TEASPOON BLACK PEPPER
1 TABLESPOON OLIVE OIL	8 EGGS, BEATEN
1 MEDIUM ONION, CHOPPED	
⅓ CUP GRATED PARMESAN CHEESE	

In medium saucepan, bring water to a boil. Add asparagus and cook 2 minutes or until tender. Drain and rinse under cold water; set aside.

In 12-inch nonstick skillet, heat oil and cook onion over medium heat 2 minutes or until tender.

Stir in asparagus, cheese, salt and pepper. Reduce heat to low and pour egg mixture into skillet. Cook covered over low heat until egg mixture sets, about 15 to 20 minutes. Do not stir.

Makes about 6 servings.

asparagus frittata

Linguine primavera

Linguine with Spring Vegetables

To make this a rustic supper staple, substitute pappardelle for the linguine.

1 TABLESPOON OLIVE OIL
1 CLOVE GARLIC, FINELY CHOPPED
½ POUND ASPARAGUS, TRIMMED AND
   CUT INTO 1-INCH PIECES
1 SMALL ONION, CHOPPED
2 MEDIUM YELLOW SQUASH AND/OR
   ZUCCHINI, SLICED

1 JAR (26 OZ.) FIVE BROTHERS™
   GRILLED SUMMER VEGETABLE SAUCE
1 PACKAGE (16 OZ.) LINGUINE PASTA,
   COOKED AND DRAINED

In large saucepan, heat oil over medium heat and cook garlic and vegetables, stirring occasionally, 5 minutes or until tender. Stir in Five Brothers™ Grilled Summer Vegetable Sauce and simmer, stirring occasionally, 5 minutes. To serve, spoon sauce over hot pasta and garnish, if desired, with grated Parmesan cheese.

Makes about 6 servings.

Penne alla puttanesca

PENNE PUTTANESCA

This classic pasta dish is an olive lover's ambrosia.

- 3 TABLESPOONS OLIVE OIL
- 2 CLOVES GARLIC, FINELY CHOPPED
- 1 JAR (26 OZ.) FIVE BROTHERS™ FRESH TOMATO BASIL SAUCE
- ½ CUP PITTED OIL-CURED OLIVES, CHOPPED
- 2 TABLESPOONS DRAINED SMALL CAPERS
- 3 ANCHOVY FILETS, DRAINED AND CHOPPED
- ½ TEASPOON DRIED OREGANO LEAVES
- ¼ TEASPOON RED PEPPER FLAKES
- ¼ TEASPOON SALT
- ¼ TEASPOON FRESHLY GROUND BLACK PEPPER
- 2 TABLESPOONS CHOPPED FRESH FLAT-LEAF ITALIAN PARSLEY
- 1 PACKAGE (16 OZ.) PENNE PASTA, COOKED AND DRAINED

In 12-inch skillet, heat oil over low heat and cook garlic 30 seconds. Add Five Brothers™ Fresh Tomato Basil Sauce, olives, capers, anchovies, oregano, red pepper flakes, salt and pepper. Simmer uncovered stirring occasionally, 15 minutes. Stir in parsley. To serve, spoon sauce over hot pasta.

Makes about 6 servings.

Insalata verde mista

MIXED GREEN SALAD WITH
OLIVE VINAIGRETTE DRESSING

The olive vinaigrette zestily dresses these exotic lettuces. Creamy Gorgonzola provides an extra little kick.

¼ CUP EXTRA-VIRGIN OLIVE OIL
1 TABLESPOON BALSAMIC VINEGAR
½ TEASPOON FINELY CHOPPED GARLIC
½ TEASPOON SALT
FRESHLY GROUND BLACK PEPPER
TO TASTE

¼ CUP PITTED RIPE OLIVES, FINELY
CHOPPED
8 CUPS MIXED SALAD GREENS
(ROMAINE, ARUGULA, RADICCHIO,
ESCAROLE, MESCLUN)
CRUMBLED GORGONZOLA CHEESE

In small bowl, with wire whisk, blend oil, vinegar, garlic, salt, pepper and olives. Spoon over chilled greens; toss lightly to coat. Garnish with cheese.

Makes about 6 servings.

Olio d'oliva

Treated like fine wine in Tuscany, olio d'oliva is the most flavorful vegetable oil. It comes in several grades, each of which relates to the degree of acidity the oil contains. The classifications include:

EXTRA VIRGIN — the finest quality, containing less than 1 percent acidity. This designation guarantees that the olives were hand picked and the oil extracted by the cold-press method (meaning, no heat or chemicals were used to speed the process)—which makes this the most expensive olive oil but also the most robust. Its color can range from greenish-golden to almost bright green; and typically, the deeper the color, the more intense the flavor. Not a cooking oil (the flavor breaks down when heated), extra virgin should be used only as a marinade, on salads, cold antipasti, topping off soups, and for a popular Tuscan treat: drizzled on slices of crusty peasant bread.

FINE VIRGIN — containing not more than 2 percent acidity, making the flavor a hint bitter. It's also paler in color. But it makes a reasonable stand-in for extra virgin (and it is not as pricey).

SEMIFINE VIRGIN AND PURE (also called Virgin) — from later pressings of olives, processed under heat or with solvents. These grades contain less than 3.3 percent and not more than 4 percent acidity, respectively. Mildly flavorful, these are best suited to sautéing, low-heat cooking, or whenever your needs call for an unassertively flavored oil.

LIGHT — not to be confused with a caloric distinction (all oil contains the same amount of calories), this labeling refers to the oil's color, fragrance, and flavor. Produced using a newer filtration process that gives it a higher smoke point than other olive oils, light is the perfect choice for frying and roasting, as well as for baking.

strawberries in balsamic vinegar

Fragole all'aceto balsamico

Strawberries in Balsamic Vinegar

*The vinegar's tartness actually brightens the fruit's flavor; and once chilled,
the vinegar loses its bite. Rinse berries before hulling so they'll absorb less water.*

4 CUPS (1 QT.) FRESH RIPE
STRAWBERRIES, STEMS REMOVED AND
HALVED LENGTHWISE

2 TABLESPOONS SUGAR
2 TABLESPOONS BALSAMIC VINEGAR

In medium bowl, toss strawberries, sugar and vinegar; chill 30 minutes. Toss just before serving and spoon into shallow dessert bowls. Garnish, if desired, with mint leaves.

Makes about 6 servings.

Grande cena neoclassica

NEOCLASSIC DINNER PARTY

*H*ere's a menu that all but guarantees a great evening. This risotto is a sophisticated crowd-pleaser (and well worth the effort). The asparagus vinaigrette—one of the season's special joys—adds a lovely splash of color. But if the mood calls for something more inspired, serve the stuffed artichoke dish instead. It's authentic Tuscan at its most savory. Serves Six.

INTINGOLO CALDO DI GRANCHI AL CARCIOFO
hot artichoke crab dip

RISOTTO TOSCANO AL POMODORO E FUNGHI
tuscan tomato mushroom risotto

POLLO ARROSTO ALLE ERBE
herb-roasted chicken

ASPARAGI VINAIGRETTE
asparagus vinaigrette

—— *or* ——

CARCIOFI RIPIENI INSAPORITI
stuffed artichokes

GELATO CON SALSA DI FRAGOLE
gelato with strawberry sauce

herb-roasted chicken

Intingolo caldo di granchi al carciofo

HOT ARTICHOKE CRAB DIP

*This deceptively simple antipasto is quite a rustic showpiece. Have it ready and
waiting when guests arrive, and you won't have to worry about making small talk.*

1 TABLESPOON OLIVE OIL

2 CLOVES GARLIC, FINELY CHOPPED

1 CAN (6 OZ.) SNOW CRABMEAT,
DRAINED

2 CUPS FIVE BROTHERS™
CREAMY ALFREDO SAUCE

1 CAN (14 OZ.) ARTICHOKE HEARTS,
DRAINED AND FINELY CHOPPED

1 PACKAGE (3 OZ.) CREAM CHEESE,
CUT INTO CHUNKS

3 TABLESPOONS CHOPPED FRESH
FLAT-LEAF ITALIAN PARSLEY (OPTIONAL)

½ TEASPOON FINELY GRATED LEMON PEEL

1 ROUND LOAF CRUSTY ITALIAN BREAD,
HOLLOWED

In medium saucepan, heat oil over medium heat and cook garlic 30 seconds. Stir in crabmeat, Five
Brothers™ Creamy Alfredo Sauce, artichoke hearts and cream cheese. Simmer over low
heat, stirring frequently, 5 minutes or until cream cheese is melted. Just before serving, stir
in parsley and lemon peel; spoon into hollowed bread. Serve hot and if desired, with sliced
Italian bread or crackers.

Makes about 3 cups dip.

Risotto toscano al pomodoro e funghi

TUSCAN TOMATO MUSHROOM RISOTTO

*By its very nature, risotto is distinctive. And this richly
hued, robust version does the Italian rice specialty proud.*

4 CANS (13-¾ OZ. EACH) BEEF BROTH
¾ CUP WATER
1 TABLESPOON UNSALTED BUTTER
2 CUPS ARBORIO OR REGULAR RICE
1 CUP FIVE BROTHERS™
   MUSHROOM & GARLIC GRILL SAUCE

¼ CUP GRATED PARMESAN CHEESE
2 TABLESPOONS CHOPPED FRESH
   FLAT-LEAF ITALIAN PARSLEY

In medium saucepan, heat broth and water; set aside. In large saucepan melt butter over medium heat, add rice and cook, stirring frequently, 3 minutes. Slowly add 1-½ cups heated broth mixture, stirring constantly. Cook over medium-low heat, stirring, until broth is absorbed. Continue adding broth, 1 cup at a time, stirring frequently until rice is slightly creamy and just tender. Stir in Five Brothers™ Mushroom & Garlic Grill Sauce, cheese and parsley.

Makes about 6 servings.

Risotto THREE RULES TO PERFECT RISOTTO

RULE 1: *Patience. Risotto is a dish that can't be rushed (but is well worth the perseverance).* RULE 2: *After adding the initial quantity of stock or other liquid, wait until all the liquid has been absorbed while stirring before adding more—and then, add only a ladleful at a time.* RULE 3: *Stir, stir, stir. And don't stop until a taste test reveals the rice tender but firm (figure on a good 25 minutes). Successfully done risotto has a creamy, porridge-like consistency.*

Erbe aromatiche

Herbs require nothing in the way of a green thumb, and the reward of having a ready-made source of the freshest seasonings is well worth the minimal time and effort. Basil grows especially quickly, as does Italian parsley. Other good bets are rosemary, sage, mint, oregano, and thyme. All you need: a sunny window, a windowsill to hold individual clay pots for each herb (or an ample enough windowbox), and seedlings of your favorite seasonings. Simply pot and water regularly. Selectively pinch or snip as needed for cooking; prune on occasion to encourage continued growth.

Pollo arrosto alle erbe

Herb-Roasted Chicken

*The combination of aromatic herbs and this creamy
Alfredo-wine sauce infuses the chicken with a nice, piquant flavor.*

2 CLOVES GARLIC

1 LEMON, HALVED

4 SPRIGS FRESH SAGE OR THYME
(OPTIONAL)

1 (7-TO-8 LB.) ROASTING CHICKEN

1 TABLESPOON OLIVE OIL

SALT AND FRESHLY GROUND BLACK PEPPER

ALFREDO-WINE SAUCE
2 CUPS FIVE BROTHERS™
CREAMY ALFREDO SAUCE
¼ CUP DRY WHITE WINE

Preheat oven to 375°. Place 1 clove garlic, lemon half and sage leaves inside chicken cavity. Rub the chicken with remaining garlic and olive oil. Squeeze remaining lemon half over chicken and season with salt and pepper. In roasting pan, on rack, arrange chicken. Roast 1 hour 45 minutes or until meat thermometer reaches 180°.

Meanwhile, prepare Alfredo-Wine Sauce. To serve, carve chicken and arrange on serving platter. Serve with Alfredo-Wine Sauce. Garnish, if desired, with fresh parsley.

ALFREDO-WINE SAUCE: In small saucepan, cook Five Brothers™ Creamy Alfredo Sauce and wine, over medium-low heat, stirring occasionally, 5 minutes or until heated through.

Makes about 6 servings.

Asparagi vinaigrette

ASPARAGUS VINAIGRETTE

*For something so sophisticated in flavor, it couldn't be simpler to make. For added
ease, prepare both asparagus and dressing a day in advance and refrigerate separately.*

2 POUNDS FRESH ASPARAGUS, TRIMMED
MIXED SALAD GREENS
¼ CUP EXTRA-VIRGIN OLIVE OIL
2 TABLESPOONS RED WINE VINEGAR
1 TABLESPOON FINELY CHOPPED FRESH
FLAT-LEAF ITALIAN PARSLEY

½ TEASPOON FINELY CHOPPED FRESH
BASIL (OPTIONAL)
¼ TEASPOON SALT
¼ TEASPOON SUGAR
⅛ TEASPOON FRESHLY GROUND
BLACK PEPPER

In 12-inch skillet, cook asparagus in boiling salted water 6 minutes or until tender. Drain and
rinse with cold water until slightly cool. On serving platter, arrange greens, then top with
asparagus; cover and refrigerate.

Meanwhile, in small bowl, blend remaining ingredients. Just before serving, pour dressing
over asparagus.

Makes about 6 servings.

Asparagi

The Care of Asparagus

- *Choosing the best-tasting asparagus is not for the colorblind. Asparagus is at its most tender when stalks are apple green and tips are purple-tinged.*

- *Look for firm stalks with moist, tightly closed tips.*

- *To prepare for cooking, snap off spears at the point where they break naturally (usually about one-quarter up from the end).*

- *Asparagus is best cooked the same day of purchase. But spears can keep in the refrigerator for up to four days.*

- *For maximum shelf life, you have two options: Wrap the ends in a damp paper towel and store spears tightly wrapped in a plastic bag in the refrigerator. Or, trim the very bottom of the stems, place spears upright in a pitcher one-quarter filled with water, and refrigerate.*

Carciofi ripieni insaporiti

STUFFED ARTICHOKES

The artichoke is the spiny passion fruit of the Tuscan garden.
And this side dish is a savory way to enjoy it.

2 TABLESPOONS OLIVE OIL
2 CLOVES GARLIC, FINELY CHOPPED
1 LARGE ONION, FINELY CHOPPED
4 CUPS FRESH BREADCRUMBS FROM
DAY-OLD ITALIAN BREAD
2 TABLESPOONS GRATED PARMESAN CHEESE
2 TABLESPOONS FINELY CHOPPED
FRESH PARSLEY

½ TEASPOON SALT
¼ TEASPOON BLACK PEPPER
⅓ CUP FIVE BROTHERS™
CREAMY ALFREDO SAUCE
4 LARGE ARTICHOKES
2 CANS (13-¾ OZ. EACH) CHICKEN
BROTH

In large skillet, heat oil over medium heat and cook garlic 30 seconds. Stir in onion and cook, stirring occasionally, 2 minutes or until tender. Stir in breadcrumbs, cheese, parsley, salt and pepper, then Five Brothers™ Creamy Alfredo Sauce; set aside.

Cut stems from artichokes and trim tips of leaves, removing tough lower leaves; rinse and drain. Spoon stuffing into center of artichokes.

In large non-aluminum saucepan, arrange artichokes; add chicken broth. Cover and bring to a boil. Reduce heat and simmer covered, basting occasionally, 1 hour or until leaves are tender and pull out easily. To serve, slice artichokes in half lengthwise.

Makes about 8 servings.

stuffed artichokes

Gelato con salsa di fragole

GELATO WITH STRAWBERRY SAUCE

An ice cream sundae for grownups!
For the most sophisticated taste, be sure the liqueur is Italian.

2 CUPS (1 PT.) FRESH OR FROZEN
STRAWBERRIES, STEMS REMOVED

5 TABLESPOONS CONFECTIONERS SUGAR

2 TABLESPOONS ANISE LIQUEUR
(OPTIONAL)

1 TEASPOON FINELY GRATED LEMON PEEL

1 QUART VANILLA GELATO
OR PREMIUM ICE CREAM

In food processor or blender, process strawberries, sugar and liqueur until smooth; stir in lemon peel; chill. To serve, scoop gelato into 6 dessert dishes; top with strawberry sauce. Garnish, if desired, with additional strawberries.

Makes about 6 servings.

gelato with strawberry sauce

Cena rustica domenicale

RUSTIC SUNDAY SUPPER

Want to feed the family's spring fever in palatable style? This menu is the cure. Starting with a full-flavored focaccia, Tuscany's favorite flat bread, there are two hearty pasta options; a tangy and colorful salad; and for dessert, the best chocolate biscotti. Here's one meal sure to keep the family around the supper table.

FOCACCIA ALLA RUCOLA E POMODORI SECCHI
focaccia with arugula and sun-dried tomatoes

ROTOLO ALLA FIORENTINA
rolled lasagna florentine

—— *or* ——

TORTELLINI ROSÉ
tortellini with tomato cream sauce

INSALATA VERDE CON ARANCE E CIPOLLE ROSSE
mixed greens with oranges and red onion salad

BISCOTTI DI CIOCCOLATO ALLE NOCI
chocolate-walnut biscotti

focaccia with arugula and sun-dried tomatoes

Focaccia alla rucola e pomodori secchi

FOCACCIA WITH ARUGULA AND SUN-DRIED TOMATOES

Cooking mellows the slightly bitter taste of arugula, a key
flavor component in this zesty, seasonal variation on basic focaccia.

BASIC FOCACCIA BREAD*
½ CUP FIVE BROTHERS™
CREAMY ALFREDO SAUCE
4 OUNCES FRESH MOZZARELLA CHEESE,
DRAINED AND SLICED
2 CLOVES GARLIC, THINLY SLICED

2 TABLESPOONS OIL-PACKED
SUN-DRIED TOMATOES
1 CUP PACKED FRESH ARUGULA, BASIL OR
SPINACH LEAVES, COARSELY CHOPPED

Preheat oven to 425°.

Spoon Five Brothers™ Creamy Alfredo Sauce over focaccia. Top with mozzarella, garlic, tomatoes and arugula. Bake 8 minutes or until cheese is melted. To serve, cut into squares.

Makes about 6 servings.

* *A recipe for homemade focaccia can be found in Volume I, however this topping works equally well on store-bought flatbread.*

Foccacia

The precursor to our modern pizza, this large, flat, rectangular or round bread has actually been around for centuries. The word itself is Latin and means "from the floor of the fireplace"—referring to the literal preparation employed by the Etruscans, who baked flat dough on the stones of the kitchen hearth. Though it never went out of style in Tuscany, focaccia has been enjoying a trendy existence here recently among restaurant chefs and recreational cooks alike—perhaps because the bread is so versatile. Pre- or post-baking, the dough can be topped, stuffed or seasoned with just about any palate-pleasing ingredient imaginable. Once baked, it can then be eaten as is—for an antipasto or snack—or sliced in half for the flavorful foundation of a panino, an Italian-style sandwich. In its purest and, many say, most satisfying form, focaccia is drizzled with olive oil and sprinkled with salt before baking—certifying that sometimes there's no need to improve on simplicity.

Rotolo alla fiorentina

ROLLED LASAGNA FLORENTINE

*The trick to this updated Italian classic is the cheese. Select only the
most full-bodied and you'll have an easy family favorite on your hands.*

- 3 TABLESPOONS BUTTER OR MARGARINE
- 1 LARGE ONION, CHOPPED
- 2 CUPS CHOPPED FRESH MUSHROOMS
- 2 OZ. PROSCIUTTO, CHOPPED (ABOUT ¼ CUP)
- 1 PACKAGE (10 OZ.) FROZEN CHOPPED SPINACH, THAWED AND SQUEEZED DRY
- 1 CUP SHREDDED MOZZARELLA CHEESE

- 1 CONTAINER (15 OZ.) RICOTTA CHEESE
- 2 EGGS
- ½ CUP GRATED PARMESAN CHEESE
- ¼ TEASPOON GROUND NUTMEG (OPTIONAL)
  SALT AND PEPPER TO TASTE
- 2 JARS (17 OZ. EACH) FIVE BROTHERS™ TOMATO ALFREDO SAUCE
- 10 LASAGNA NOODLES, COOKED

Preheat oven to 375°. In large skillet, melt butter and cook onion and mushrooms over medium heat, stirring occasionally, until liquid from mushrooms cooks off. Remove from heat; stir in remaining ingredients except lasagna noodles and Five Brothers™ Tomato Alfredo Sauce. Spread half-cup vegetable cheese filling over each lasagna noodle, roll to enclose filling; set aside.

In 13 x 9-inch baking dish, spread ½ cup Five Brothers™ Tomato Alfredo Sauce. Arrange stuffed lasagna rolls seam side down in dish, cover and bake 30 minutes or until bubbling. Serve with remaining Five Brothers™ Tomato Alfredo Sauce, heated.

Makes about 6 servings.

rolled lasagna florentine

tortellini with tomato cream sauce

Tortellini rosé

Tortellini with Tomato Cream Sauce

*Subtle flavorings, substantial pasta and simple preparation
make this the perfect choice for a casual supper anytime.*

1 PACKAGE (16 OZ.) FRESH OR FROZEN
   TORTELLINI, COOKED AND DRAINED
2 CUPS FIVE BROTHERS™
   FRESH TOMATO BASIL SAUCE

¾ CUP LIGHT CREAM OR
   HALF AND HALF

In medium saucepan, heat Five Brothers™ Fresh Tomato Basil Sauce. Stir in cream and remove from heat. Serve over hot tortellini. Garnish, if desired, with shaved Parmesan cheese.

Makes about 6 servings.

Insalata verde con arance e cipolle rosse

MIXED GREENS WITH ORANGES AND RED ONION SALAD

Both delicious and decorative, this aromatic salad is a
palate-pleasing foil to rich, cheesy pasta dishes.

8 CUPS ASSORTED MIXED SALAD GREENS
2 MEDIUM ORANGES, PEELED AND CUT
  INTO SECTIONS
1 SMALL RED ONION, THINLY SLICED
1/4 CUP EXTRA-VIRGIN OLIVE OIL

3 TABLESPOONS BALSAMIC VINEGAR
1 TABLESPOON HONEY
1/4 TEASPOON SALT
1/4 TEASPOON BLACK PEPPER

In large salad bowl, combine greens, oranges and onion; set aside. In small bowl, with wire whisk, blend oil, vinegar, honey, salt and pepper; drizzle over salad.

Makes about 6 servings.

mixed greens with oranges and red onion salad

Biscotti di cioccolato alle noci

CHOCOLATE-WALNUT BISCOTTI

*The raves these superior Italian cookies garner—from adults
to kids alike—make them more than worth the little extra effort.*

2 CUPS CHOPPED WALNUTS
3 SQUARES (1 OZ. EACH)
   UNSWEETENED BAKING CHOCOLATE
⅓ CUP UNSALTED BUTTER
2 CUPS ALL-PURPOSE FLOUR

2 TEASPOONS BAKING POWDER
3 LARGE EGGS
1 CUP SUGAR
2 TEASPOONS FINELY GRATED
   ORANGE PEEL

Preheat oven to 350°. On cookie sheet, toast walnuts 10 minutes or until golden brown; set aside.

In small saucepan, melt chocolate and butter over very low heat, stirring occasionally. Remove from heat and stir until smooth; let cool.

In small bowl, sift flour and baking powder; set aside. In large bowl, beat eggs lightly. Gradually add sugar, beating until light and fluffy. Stir in cooled chocolate mixture, then flour mixture until well blended. Stir in walnuts and orange peel. Divide dough in half, wrap in plastic and chill at least 1 hour.

On greased baking sheet, form each dough half into a flattened log, each about 14-inches long x 2-½-inches wide. Place 4 inches apart on baking sheet. Bake 40 minutes or until logs are firm when pressed in the center.

Remove from oven. On a cutting board, cut logs crosswise on the diagonal into ½-inch slices. Arrange biscotti cut-side down on baking sheet. Bake 10 minutes or until crisp. On wire rack, cool completely. Store in airtight container up to 1 week.

Makes about 3 dozen biscotti.

chocolate-walnut biscotti

La pasta nella cucina toscana

PASTA OF THE TUSCAN KITCHEN

The word "pasta" means paste in Italian and refers to the dough made by combining semolina (durum wheat flour that is more coarsely ground than regular wheat flours) with water. Its origin is actually unknown; what is known, however, is that pasta, with its many appetizing flavors, has been central to the Tuscan table for centuries. And while this modest food group comes in literally hundreds of shapes, sizes, and thicknesses (more than 350, in fact), the following 21—which include both dried pasta and fresh (those that have eggs added to the dough)—are among the most popular and interesting.

Although every pasta is special, there's no sacrilege in substitution. For the most part, you may feel confident about swapping one similarly-sized pasta for another without fear of sabotaging a dish's integrity.

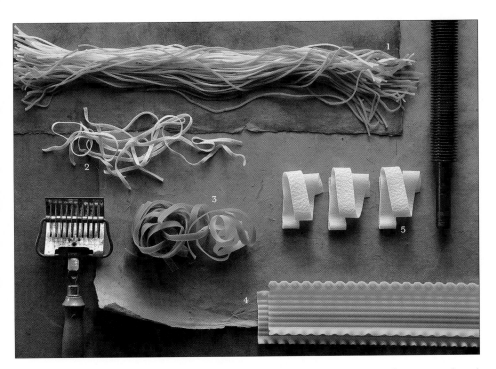

1. LINGUINE — "little tongues"; long, narrow noodles, about ⅛-inch wide that work best with clinging sauces (think pesto or cream-based). A southern Italian pasta, linguine are rarely used in Tuscany; Tuscans favor spaghetti instead.

2. TAGLIATELLE —Tuscan favorites, long, flat strips, about ¼-inch wide (tagliolini are thinner).

3. FETTUCCINE — "little ribbons"; long, flat egg noodles, about ⅜-inch wide, that can stand up to the most substantial red or white sauces. It is a commonly used pasta in Tuscany and a specialty of Bologna, where they're traditionally served with a meat-based sauce.

4. LASAGNE — flat, 2-inch broad strips of egg-noodle dough, often cut with a serrated pastry wheel for a ruffled edge.

5. PAPPARDELLE — the most Tuscan of pastas, broad egg noodles, about ½-inch wide, traditionally paired with game sauces, though any hearty meat sauce works well.

6. FUSILLI — short corkscrew shapes or long, curly strands that go well with thick creamy sauces, adorned with meat or vegetables. Unlike spaghetti, long fusilli do not work so well with simple oil-based sauces.

7. SPAGHETTI AND SPAGHETTINI — "strings"; the most well-known pasta, especially good with oil-based sauces that incorporate seafood or vegetables. In Italy, spaghetti are never served with meatballs—that's an American invention.

8. BUCATINI (also known as perciatelli) — long, thick, hollow noodles that work best with zesty tomato-based sauces.

9. VERMICELLI — "little worms"; long strands, thinner than spaghetti, that are best suited to simple oil-based or delicate sauces.

10. CAPELLI D'ANGELO (also called capellini) —"angel hair"; long, delicate noodles that serve up best with light sauces or broth.

11. PASTINE — a variety of miniature pastas, including annellini ("little rings"), ditalini ("little thimbles"), orzo ("barley"), tubetti ("little tubes"), and stelline ("little stars"), that are most often served in clear broth soups.

12. RAVIOLI — the classic stuffed pasta, these square pillows of egg-noodle dough are filled with various stuffings of meat, cheese, or vegetables and best served with simple tomato sauce.

13. ORECCHIETTE — "little ears"; small, round, slightly concave shapes. A specialty of Apulia, commonly served with a sauce of broccoli florets, olive oil, and anchovies.

14. CONCHIGLIE — "shells"; oblong shell shapes, pinched at the ends. They pair well with meat sauces and vegetables.

15. TORTELLINI — "little twists"; small, ring-shaped egg-noodle dumplings. A specialty of Bologna, traditionally stuffed with a meat or cheese filling and able to stand up to cream-based and hearty tomato sauces.

16. FARFALLE —"butterflies"; bowtie-shaped pastas that are the perfect foil for light sauces studded with vegetables.

17. ZITI — "bridegrooms"; smooth, straight-cut tubular shapes, narrower than rigatoni but can accommodate the same types of sauces; often served baked in a tomato sauce with cheese.

18. RADIATORI — "radiators"; stubby spirals best suited to chunky sauces; also a good choice for cold pasta salad.

19. ROTINI — short, thin spirals that can handle the same types of sauces as radiatori and rotelle.

20. PENNE — "quills"; short, hollow tubular shapes cut on the diagonal. (When ridged, they're called penne rigate.) These versatile noodles work as well with robust, chunky sauces as with the simplest tomato sauce.

21. RIGATONI — stubby, grooved tube shapes, larger and less delicate than penne, that stand up well to robust meat- or cream-based sauces.

Share the Passion!
Join the Five Brothers Culinary Club

Send us your name and address on a $3\frac{1}{2}$ x 5 card and you will periodically receive our free newsletter filled with inventive recipes and creative food ideas for unforgettable home meals.

Mail to: FIVE BROTHERS CULINARY CLUB
P.O. BOX 1210-B
GRAND RAPIDS, MN 55745-1210